# I Like Making
# Tamales

Written by Allison Pomenta
Illustrated by Kristin Barr

McGraw Hill **Wright Group**

The **McGraw·Hill** Companies

Illustrations:
The McGraw-Hill Companies, Inc./Kristin Barr

---

**www.WrightGroup.com**

 **Wright Group**

Printed in Mexico.

Send all inquiries to:
Wright Group/McGraw-Hill
P.O. Box 812960
Chicago, IL 60681

ISBN 978-0-07-658182-5
MHID 0-07-658182-9

4 5 6 7 8 9  DRN  16 15 14 13 12 11

Mama is going to make tamales.
I love tamales!

I am going to help Mama.

We have a lot of corn husks here!
I'll pick the best ones to use
for cooking.

If the corn husk is bigger
than my hand, it's the right size.

If it is smaller than my hand,
it's not big enough to make a tamale.

All of these corn husks are bigger
than my hand.

But they are smaller
than Mama's hand.

At school we use connecting cubes
to measure things.

How big is my hand?

How big is Mama's hand?
"Mama?"
"Yes, Kiko."

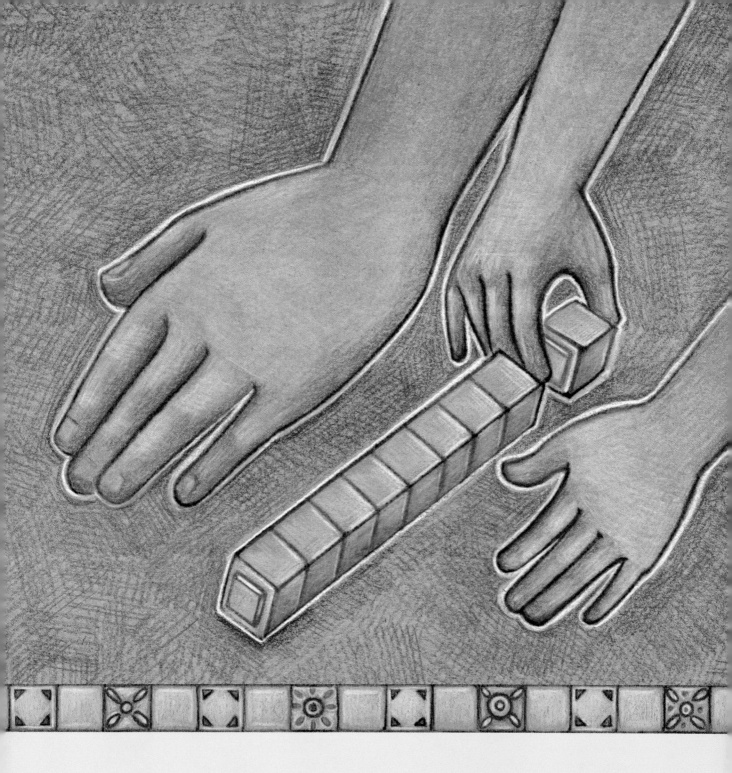

"See what I can do!"

"Kiko, we have a lot of corn husks to make a lot of tamales!"

14

That's good news
because I love tamales!

I get the tamale pot out for Mama.
It's big, but I can carry it.

"Kiko, bring me the corn flour, please."
"Mama, it is heavy. But I can carry
it."

"You can use the balance
to see which is heavier."

The corn flour is heavier!

Mama is making the dough.
What can I do?

"I'm going to use a cup to measure the right amount of broth."

Mama shows me how to fill
the corn husks.

And how to fold them to make
tamale packages.

"Mama?"
"Yes, Kiko."
"Look how many we made!"

What can I do while the tamales cook?

I show Mama how to use our feet
to see how big the kitchen is.

"Are the tamales ready?"
"Not yet, Kiko."

What else can I do?

"Why don't you use your hand lens
to look at some corn husks?"

"Look at that!"

"Kiko?"
"Yes, Mama."
"Come eat tamales."
"Yum!"